True Survival

ABBY SUNDERLAND

LOST
AT
SEA

Virginia Loh-Hagan

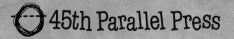
45th Parallel Press

Published in the United States of America by Cherry Lake Publishing
Ann Arbor, Michigan
www.cherrylakepublishing.com

Reading Adviser: Marla Conn MS, Ed., Literacy specialist, Read-Ability, Inc.
Book Cover Design: Felicia Macheske

Photo Credits: ©Voyagerix/Shutterstock.com, cover; ©GABRIEL BOUYS/AFP/Getty Images, 5; ©miljko/
iStock.com, 7; ©Nikolia Apostolou/Shutterstock.com, 8; ©fstop123/iStock.com, 11; ©Franck Boston/
Shutterstock.com, 12; ©De Visu/Shutterstock.com, 14; ©maradon 333/Shutterstock.com, 17; ©Jamie Stamey/
iStock.com, 19; ©airn/Shutterstock.com, 20; ©brickrena/Shutterstock.com, 23; ©VM_Studio/iStock.com, 24;
©Andrea Izzotti/Shutterstock.com, 27; ©AP Photo/Reed Saxon, 29

Graphic Elements Throughout: ©Gordan/Shutterstock.com; ©adike/Shutterstock.com; ©Yure/Shutterstock.com

45th Parallel Press is an imprint of Cherry Lake Publishing.

Library of Congress Cataloging-in-Publication Data
Names: Loh-Hagan, Virginia, author.
Title: Abby Sunderland : lost at sea / by Virginia Loh-Hagan.
Description: Ann Arbor, Michigan : Cherry Lake Publishing, 2019. | Series: True survival |
    Includes bibliographical references and index. | Audience: Grade 4 to 6.
Identifiers: LCCN 2018035187 | ISBN 9781534143326 (hardcover) | ISBN 9781534139886 (pbk.) |
    ISBN 9781534141087 (pdf) | ISBN 9781534142282 (hosted ebook)
Subjects: LCSH: Sunderland, Abby, 1993—Juvenile literature. | Survival at sea—Juvenile literature. |
    Women sailors—United States—Biography—Juvenile literature. | Women adventurers—United States—
    Biography—Juvenile literature.
Classification: LCC GV810.92.S86 L64 2019 | DDC 797.1092 [B]—dc23LC record available at
    https://lccn.loc.gov/2018035187

Cherry Lake Publishing would like to acknowledge the work of The Partnership for 21st Century Skills.
Please visit *www.p21.org* for more information.

Printed in the United States of America
Corporate Graphics

table of contents

chapter one

Like Brother, Like Sister

Who is Abby Sunderland? Who is Zac Sunderland?

Abby Sunderland was born on October 19, 1993. She's an American sailor. In 2010, she tried to set a world record. She wanted to be the youngest person to sail **solo** around the world, without stopping. Solo means alone. It means without help. Sunderland didn't do this. But her story of survival made her famous.

Sunderland is from Thousand Oaks, California. Her parents are Marianne and Laurence Sunderland.

They have eight children. Sunderland is the second oldest. She was **homeschooled**. This means that she was taught at home. Her parents were her teachers. Marianne taught school subjects. Laurence built boats. He taught his children about sailing.

The Sunderland family lives in Southern California.

spotlight *biography*

Jessica Watson is from Australia. She's a sailor. She's the youngest to sail solo nonstop around the world. She did this at age 16. She did this in 2010. She sailed for 210 days alone at sea. Her boat is called *Ella's Pink Lady*. Australia's leader called her a hero. She said she wasn't. She said she was an "ordinary person who had a dream, worked hard at it, and proved that anything really is possible." She did other great things. She led a team that competed in a boat race. She was the youngest to compete. She got an award for being the first female captain. She also does community service. She's the Youth Ambassador for the United Nations World Food Program. She traveled to refugee camps. She has dyslexia. This means she has a hard time reading. But that doesn't stop her. She wrote a blog. She wrote books. She did a film about her experience.

Sunderland grew up sailing. She'd live on a sailboat. She helped her father deliver boats to people. She sailed up and down the California coast. She trained in ocean sailing. She trained with experienced sailors.

When she was 13, she decided she wanted to sail the world. Her father trained her. He tested her. One day, they were training. They sailed for 20 hours. He said, "It was a particularly rough day. And her boat was rocking . . . I knew she was freezing cold, tired, and hungry." Her father asked if she still wanted to sail around the world. Sunderland said, "Where is my boat?" She was determined!

The Sunderland family sailed to Australia, New Zealand, the United Kingdom, and Mexico.

She wanted to be like her older brother. Actually, she wanted to beat him. Zac Sunderland set a world record. He was the first person under the age of 18 to sail solo around the world. He did this at age 17. He did this in 2009. He sailed for 13 months and 2 days. He stopped at different places. He sailed through lightning storms. He had to fix broken boat parts. He even dealt with **pirates**. Pirates are robbers who steal from ships. But Zac's trip was pretty safe.

Zac held the record for 42 days. Mike Perham beat Zac's record. Then Perham's record was beat by Jessica Watson. Abby Sunderland wanted to beat them all.

◄ Zac's first bed was a basket in a boat.

chapter two

Getting Ready

What was in Sunderland's ditch bag? What were her challenges? How did she overcome her challenges?

Zac gave Sunderland his **ditch bag**. All good sailors have ditch bags. These are strong, waterproof bags. They keep things dry. Sailors pack things they need to survive on a lifeboat. Ditch bags are for when things go wrong. Sunderland packed blankets. She packed a diving mask. She packed flippers. She packed emergency radios. She packed a water kit. She packed food. She packed a medical kit. She packed a flashlight. She packed **flares**. Flares are bright lights. They're used to signal for help.

Sunderland wanted to go faster than Zac. She wanted to sail a harder path. She wanted to do her trip without stopping.

Ditch bags are also called "abandon ship" bags.

She had many challenges. First, the trip would cost a lot of money. Her family didn't have a lot of money. Second, she had limited experience sailing alone in open seas. After all, she was hardly ever alone. She always had family members with her. Third, she'd have to eat **freeze-dried** food. This food is dried. Water is taken out. It's meant to last a long time. Fourth, she could only sleep for a little while. She had to be strapped to a small bed. Fifth, she didn't know how to fix engines. Sailors who travel for a long time know how to fix boat parts. Sixth, she could die.

Sunderland's bed was like a narrow plank of wood.

explained by science

Some sailboats are sleek and fast. They can travel three times faster than the speed of wind. How can they do this? In physics, there is an important idea. It's the conservation of energy. Conservation means to save. Sailboats can't make energy. They use energy from more than one kind of wind. They work like airplanes use the flow of air to fly. Imagine riding a bike. The air may be still. But you feel wind as you go faster. This is called "apparent wind." It's the wind we feel when in motion. True wind is wind we feel when standing still. Sailboats use true and apparent winds. True wind pushes the sailboat. Apparent wind pulls or drags it forward. This drag is a force. It's called lift. Lift helps a sailboat move faster than the true wind. Lift also helps an airplane fly.

Nothing stopped her. Sunderland said, "It's always been a dream." She got **sponsors**. Sponsors pay for people. They support people. Sunderland was able to get a sailboat. She named it *Wild Eyes*. It was fast. It was a racing boat. It was a **sloop**. Sloops have only one **mast**. Masts are poles that hold sails.

She planned for safety. She had sailing tools. She had a **satellite** phone. Satellites orbit the earth. Sunderland could call for help from anywhere. She could call her parents to check in. She could call a team of sailing experts. This team could give her tips when needed.

◀ Sunderland's sailboat was 40 feet (12 meters) long.

chapter three

Alone at Sea

When did Sunderland finally set sail? What happened to her while sailing?

Sunderland set sail on January 23, 2010. She started later than she wanted to. The weather was getting more dangerous. Seas would have more moving ice. There'd be more storms. But Sunderland didn't want to wait for a safer time. She needed to be the youngest. She was already 17. She said, "If I don't have a record, I don't have media attention and I don't get my trip **funded**." Funded means paid for.

She sailed from Marina del Rey in California. She had trouble after a few days. She had problems with her boat. So, she stopped in Cabo San Lucas in Mexico.

She got gas. She got batteries. She fixed her sailboat. She set sail again on February 6.

She crossed the **equator** on February 19. The equator is the line that divides the earth into northern and southern parts.

Wild Eyes alone cost $90,000.

would you?

- **Would you want to set a world record?**
  People who set records can become famous. There
  can be news stories about them. But not everyone
  can set records. Competition is tough. Each year,
  50,000 people apply to Guinness World Records.
  Only 1,000 are celebrated. Once you set a record,
  someone else can break it. It never ends.

- **Would you travel alone?** Some people like to
  travel alone. They can be on their own schedules.
  They can meet new people. But traveling with
  others can be fun.

- **Would you want to be homeschooled?** There
  are about 2 million students learning at home. These
  students learn at their own pace. Their parents are
  their teachers. Not all parents can do this. Teaching
  takes a lot of time and work.

She rounded Cape Horn on March 31. This is the most southern point of South America. It's known as the "graveyard of the sea." She became the youngest solo sailor to do this. She faced rough water. She faced heavy winds.

A month later, she sailed to Africa. She needed to fix her boat. She landed in South Africa. She had to give up the "nonstop" part of her record goal. She set sail again on May 21.

The Atlantic, Pacific, and Southern Oceans meet at Cape Horn.

A couple of days later, a line got stuck near the top of her mast. Sunderland tried to climb the mast. But it was too dangerous. She had to sail through the night without full power of her sails.

Sunderland was deep in the southern Indian Ocean. It has dangerous waters. There were big storms. There were big winds. There were big waves. Her sailboat was knocked over. Icy water threw Sunderland across her boat. She blacked out. When she woke up, she faced big problems. Her mast was broken. She couldn't sail. She lost her satellite phone. She had no way of calling for help. She was lost at sea. This happened around June 10.

◄ Her mast was 60 feet (18.3 m) tall. It snapped like a twig because of the rough seas.

chapter four

Saved by Technology

How was Sunderland rescued?
When was she rescued?

Sunderland set off two emergency radio **beacons**. Beacons are devices. They send out information. The beacons were made by NASA. NASA is the National Aeronautics and Space Administration. The beacons sent a help signal to a special satellite. This satellite was 22,500 miles (36,210 kilometers) away in space. It's designed for search and rescue. It located Sunderland. It sent her location to rescue groups around the world.

The U.S. Coast Guard contacted Sunderland's parents. Her parents said, "Abby has all of the equipment on board to survive a crisis like this. She has a dry suit, survival suit, life raft, and ditch bag with emergency supplies. If she can keep warm and hang on, help will be there as soon as possible."

The nearest ship to her was 400 miles (644 km) away.

Sunderland was over 2,000 nautical miles from Perth, Australia.

Australian officials sent a rescue jet. The jet reached the search zone. It found Sunderland's boat in about 10 minutes. It made radio contact with Sunderland. French officials sent rescue ships. The captain of one of the boats fell into the water. He had to be rescued.

Sunderland was rescued on June 12. This was two days after she set off the beacons. She said, "I was expecting it to be weeks. When you set off your beacon, you know someone is going to hear you. But I wasn't sure if I was going to be helped. But I don't think it could have been done any faster."

survival tips

TRAPPED ALONE!

- Keep sane. Being alone for a long time could make you see or hear things that aren't there. Try to stay focused on reality.

- Keep your mind busy. Recite the alphabet. Sing songs. Whistle. Test yourself on things you know.

- Keep yourself busy. Gather food. Build shelter. Make tools. Take your mind off being lonely.

- Learn to respond to danger. Learn to adapt to new things. Mental skills are important for survival.

- Have a positive attitude. Have a strong will to live. Have hope. Never give up.

- Rest. Save your energy. This will keep your mind sharp. If you're tired, you make bad choices.

- Control your fears. Don't panic. Make plans instead.

chapter five

Storm on Land

What happened to Sunderland's sailboat? What were the controversies around Sunderland's trip?

Sunderland's father said, "We are just really excited and **ecstatic** that Abigail is in safe hands. She was in good spirits." Ecstatic means happy.

But *Wild Eyes* wasn't in safe hands. It was left in the open seas. It was sinking.

Sunderland said, "Overall, it's the best experience of my life." She still wants to sail around the world. She's also taking flying lessons. She could fly around the world one day.

She was rescued from the stormy seas. But there were many stories about her trip. Many people were unhappy about what happened.

There were issues about the cost of the rescue. The rescue cost $200,000 to $300,000. French and Australian citizens paid for it.

Many ships are sunk in the Indian Ocean.

Rest in Peace

A tsunami is a dangerous sea storm. It's a series of strong ocean waves. The Indian Ocean tsunami of 2004 was huge. It was one of the deadliest natural disasters in history. It started with a big earthquake under the sea. It happened on December 26, 2004. It triggered tsunamis that hit countries by the Indian Ocean. The countries with the most damage were Indonesia, Sri Lanka, India, and Thailand. Tsunamis hit these areas for 7 hours. They hit as far as East Africa. The waves were 100 feet (30.5 m) high. They covered 100 feet (30.5 m) of land. They wiped out cities. It caused 280,000 deaths. One-third of the deaths were children. Children couldn't escape the waves. Four times more women died. Women were waiting on beaches for fishermen to return home.

Some people thought Sunderland was too young. They thought the trip was too dangerous. They blamed her parents. They thought the parents were careless.

Some people questioned Sunderland's choices. They thought she had the wrong type of boat. They thought she was in the wrong place. They knew the Indian Ocean could be dangerous. They thought she sailed at the wrong time. They questioned her skills.

But Sunderland said she knew what she was doing. She understands the ocean. She understands the dangers. She's lucky to be alive.

Some people blamed Sunderland's parents for putting her in danger.

Did You Know?

- Sunderland was featured in a documentary. Documentaries are movies about real people and events. The documentary was called *Wild Eyes: The Abby Sunderland Story*. It was produced and directed by Sunderland's father.

- Sunderland wrote a book about her survival. She did this in 2011. The book's title is *Unsinkable: A Young Woman's Courageous Battle on the High Seas*. It's co-written by Lynn Vincent.

- Sunderland was in the 4-H Club. At age 9, she bred and raised rabbits, chickens, and turkeys. She sold them for money. She won prizes.

- On February 27, 2010, people were worried about Sunderland's safety. There was an earthquake in Chile. But Sunderland was far enough away. She wasn't affected by it.

- Sunderland left Cape Town, South Africa, on Friday, May 21, 2010. Sailors have a superstition. They don't like sailing on Fridays. They think it's bad luck.

- On October 25, 2010, Sunderland went to a NASA office. She met the engineers who made the beacons.

- In 2011, Zac and Laurence Sunderland were in *The Amazing Race*. They took sixth place.

- The Sunderlands' eighth child was born one day after Abby arrived back in the United States. They named the boy Paul-Louis. Paul Louis Le Moigne is the name of the French captain who rescued Sunderland.

Consider This!

Take a Position: Many people were upset at Sunderland's parents. They didn't think parents should let their kids travel around the world by themselves. They thought the trip was unsafe. Do you think her parents were right or wrong? Argue your point with reasons and evidence.

Say What? Read the 45th Parallel Press book about Harrison Okene. Compare it to Sunderland. Explain how they're alike. Explain how they're different.

Think About It! Sunderland was inspired by her older brother. Is there someone who inspires you? How so? What are you going to do about it?

Learn More

- Sunderland, Abby, and Lynn Vincent. *Unsinkable: A Young Woman's Courageous Battle on the High Seas*. Nashville, TN: Thomas Nelson, 2011.

- Uhl, Xina M. *Abby Sunderland: Alone on the Indian Ocean*. Mankato, MN: Child's World, 2016.

Glossary

beacons (BEE-kuhnz) lights used as signals

ditch bag (DICH BAG) a waterproof bag of emergency supplies needed in case sailors have to abandon ships

ecstatic (ek-STAT-ik) really happy

equator (ih-KWAY-tur) the imaginary line that separates the world into the Northern and Southern Hemispheres

flares (FLAIRZ) bright lights used to signal for help

freeze-dried (FREEZ DRYD) processed food that can be stored for a long time because the water is taken out

funded (FUHND-id) paid for

homeschooled (HOME-skoold) taught at home most likely by parents rather than at school

mast (MAST) tall pole that holds up sails

pirates (PYE-rits) robbers who go on board ships and take things

satellite (SAT-uh-lite) communication device that orbits the earth

sloop (SLOOP) a type of sailboat with one mast

solo (SOH-loh) alone without assistance

sponsors (SPAHN-surz) people or groups that support ideas by paying for them

Index

About the Author

Dr. Virginia Loh-Hagan is an author, university professor, and former classroom teacher. She prefers swimming in her pool to sailing the oceans. She lives in San Diego with her very tall husband and very naughty dogs. To learn more about her, visit www.virginialoh.com.